Music Gone Wild
Song Book

Frances Turnbull

Music Gone Wild Song Book
All rights reserved
Musicaliti Publishing, Bolton, UK

ISBN: 978-1907935688

Contents

Ukulele Chords

Ukuleles are small, accessible and relatively cheap instruments that can be used to play the accompaniment to many songs.

Each string should be tuned to specific notes (can be found on tuned instruments like xylophones, pianos or recorders etc.). The standard ukulele tuning is:

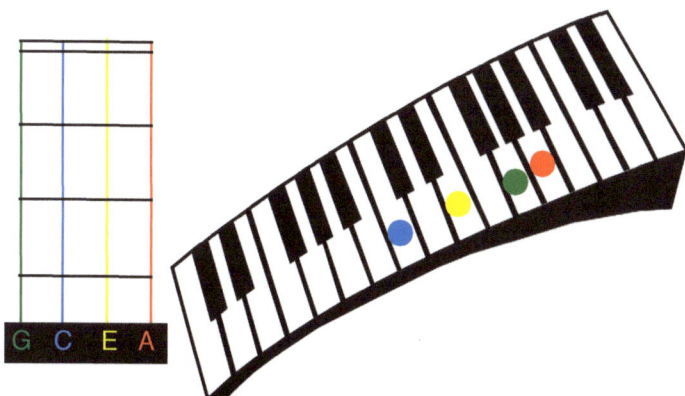

G C E A

God Can't Eat Ants

By placing your fingers on the frets at the positions on the pictures, (between the lines), you change the sound of the strings into chords when strummed altogether.

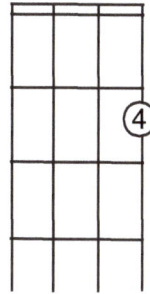

C

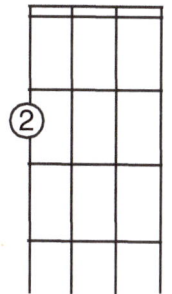

Am

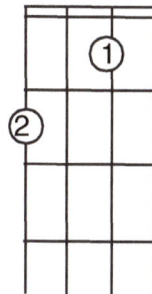

F

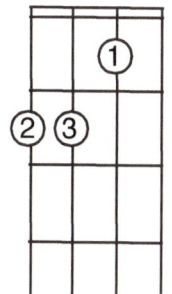

Dm

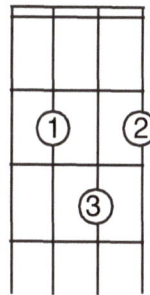

G

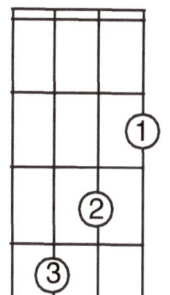

Em

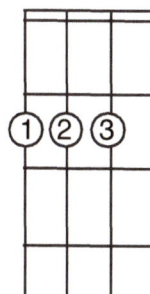

D

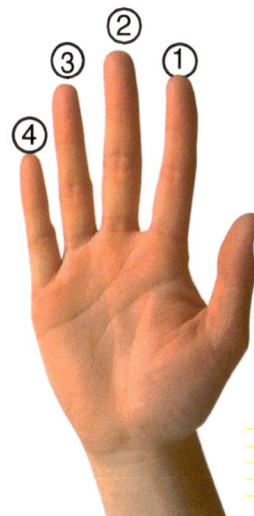

🎵 usicaliti

🎵 usicaliti

Frances Turnbull

A Place in the Choir

Traditional

All God's creatures have a place in the choir
Some sing lower, some sing higher
Some sing out loud on a telephone wire
Some just clap their hands or paws
Or anything they got now!

Listen to the bass, the one at the bottom
Where the bullfrog croaks and the hippopotamus
Moans and groans with a big to-do
And the old coyote howls

Singing in the night time, singing in the day
The little duck quacks and he's on his way
The possum ain't got much to say
And the porcupine talks to himself

The dogs and cats are gonna take up the middle
Where the honeybee hums and the crickets fiddle
The donkey brays and the pony neighs
And the old mad dingo howls

Listen to the top, where the little birds sing
All the melodies with the high notes ringing
The hoot owl hollers over everything
And the jaybird disagrees

It's a simple song of living sung everywhere
By the ox and the fox and the grizzly bear
The grumpy alligator and the hawk above
The sly raccoon and the turtle dove

Bill Staines

♫♪usicalitti ♫♪usicalitti

Ants Go Marching

Traditional

The ants go marching 1 by 1, hurrah, hurrah!
The ants go marching 1 by 1, hurrah, hurrah!
The ants go marching 1 by 1
The little one stops to suck his thumb
And they all go marching down into the
Ground to get out of the rain!

The ants go marching 2 by 2, hurrah, hurrah!
The ants go marching 2 by 2, hurrah, hurrah!
The ants go marching 2 by 2
The little one stops to tie his shoe
And they all go marching down into the
Ground to get out of the rain!

The ants go marching 3 by 3, hurrah, hurrah!
The ants go marching 3 by 3, hurrah, hurrah!
The ants go marching 3 by 3
The little one stops to climb a tree
And they all go marching down into the
Ground to get out of the rain!

The ants go marching 4 by 4, hurrah, hurrah!
The ants go marching 4 by 4, hurrah, hurrah!
The ants go marching 4 by 4
The little one stops to knock on the door
And they all go marching down into the
Ground to get out of the rain!

The ants go marching 5 by 5, hurrah, hurrah!
The ants go marching 5 by 5, hurrah, hurrah!
The ants go marching 5 by 5
The little one stops to give a high five
And they all go marching down into the
Ground to get out of the rain!

The ants go marching 6 by 6, hurrah, hurrah!
The ants go marching 6 by 6, hurrah, hurrah!
The ants go marching 6 by 6
The little one stops to do some tricks
And they all go marching down into the
Ground to get out of the rain!

The ants go marching 7 by 7, hurrah, hurrah!
The ants go marching 7 by 7, hurrah, hurrah!
The ants go marching 7 by 7
The little one stops to go to heaven
And they all go marching down into the
Ground to get out of the rain!

The ants go marching 8 by 8, hurrah, hurrah!
The ants go marching 8 by 8, hurrah, hurrah!
The ants go marching 8 by 8
The little one stops to see if he's late
And they all go marching down into the
Ground to get out of the rain!

The ants go marching 9 by 9, hurrah, hurrah!
The ants go marching 9 by 9, hurrah, hurrah!
The ants go marching 9 by 9
The little one stops to look divine
And they all go marching down into the
Ground to get out of the rain!

The ants go marching 10 by 10, hurrah, hurrah!
The ants go marching 10 by 10, hurrah, hurrah!
The ants go marching 10 by 10
The little one stops to do it again
And they all go marching down into the
Ground to get out of the rain!

musicaliti

musicaliti

Frances Turnbull

Green Grass

Traditional

There was a hole down in the ground
The prettiest hole that you ever did see
Oh, the hole in the ground
And the green grass grew all around, all around
And the green grass grew all around
And the green grass grew all around, all around
And the green grass grew all around

Now in that hole there was a tree
The prettiest tree that you ever did see
Oh, the tree in the hole
and the hole in the ground
And the green grass grew all around, all around
And the green grass grew all around
And the green grass grew all around, all around
And the green grass grew all around

Now in that tree there was a branch
The prettiest branch that you ever did see
Oh, the branch in the tree,
and the tree in the hole,
and the hole in the ground
And the green grass grew all around, all around
And the green grass grew all around
And the green grass grew all around, all around
And the green grass grew all around

Now in that branch there was a bough
The prettiest bough that you ever did see
Oh, the bough in the branch,
and the branch in the tree,
and the tree in the hole,
and the hole in the ground
And the green grass grew all around, all around
And the green grass grew all around
And the green grass grew all around, all around
And the green grass grew all around

Now in that bough there was a twig
The prettiest twig that you ever did see
Oh, the twig in the bough,
and the bough in the branch,
and the branch in the tree,
and the tree in the hole,
and the hole in the ground
And the green grass grew all around, all around
And the green grass grew all around
And the green grass grew all around, all around
And the green grass grew all around

Now on that twig there was a nest
The prettiest nest that you ever did see
Oh, the nest in the twig,
and the twig in the bough,
and the bough in the branch,
and the branch in the tree,
and the tree in the hole,
and the hole in the ground
And the green grass grew all around, all around
And the green grass grew all around
And the green grass grew all around, all around
And the green grass grew all around

Now in that nest there was an egg
The prettiest egg that you ever did see
Oh, the egg in the nest
and the nest in the twig,
and the twig in the bough,
and the bough in the branch,
and the branch in the tree,
and the tree in the hole,
and the hole in the ground
And the green grass grew all around, all around
And the green grass grew all around
And the green grass grew all around, all around
And the green grass grew all around

Green Grass

Traditional

Now in that **C** egg there was a bird
The prettiest bird that you ever did **G** see
Oh, the **C** bird in the egg and the egg in the nest,
and the nest in the twig, and the twig in the bough,
and the bough in the branch,
and the **C** branch in the tree, and the tree in the hole,
and the hole in the ground
And the **C** green grass grew all around, all around **G**
And the **C** green grass grew all around
And the **C** green grass grew all around, all around
And the **C** green grass grew all around

Now on that **C** bird there was a wing
The prettiest wing that you ever did **G** see
Oh, the **C** wing on the bird and the bird in the egg,
and the **C** egg in the nest, and the nest in the twig,
and the **C** twig in the bough,
and the **C** bough in the branch,
and the **C** branch in the tree, and the tree in the hole,
and the **C** hole in the ground
And the **C** green grass grew all around, all around **F**
And the **C** green grass grew all around
And the **C** green grass grew all around, all around
And the **C** green grass grew all around

Now on that **C** wing there was a feather
The prettiest feather that you ever did **G** see
Oh, the **C** feather on the wing,
and the **C** wing on the bird, and the bird in the egg,
and the **C** egg in the nest, and the nest in the twig,
and the **C** twig in the bough,
and the **C** bough in the branch,
and the **C** branch in the tree, and the tree in the hole,
and the **C** hole in the ground
And the **C** green grass grew all around, all around **F**
And the **C** green grass grew all around
And the **C** green grass grew all around, all around **F**
And the **C** green grass grew all around

Now on that **C** feather there was a flea
The prettiest flea that you ever did see **G**
Oh, the **C** flea on the feather,
and the feather on the wing,
and the wing on the bird,
and the **C** bird in the egg,
and the egg in the nest,
and the nest in the twig,
and the twig in the bough,
and the bough in the branch,
and the branch in the tree,
and the **C** tree in the hole,
and the hole in the ground
And the **C** green grass grew all around,
all around
And the **C** green grass grew all around
And the **C** green grass grew all around,
all around **F**
And the **C** green grass grew all around

* * *

Pictures on page 26-27
at the
back of the book
to cut out
and use
for this song!

* * *

usicaliti

usicaliti

Over in the Meadow

Traditional

Over in the meadow in the sand in the sun
Lived an old mother tiger
And her little tiger ONE
ROAR, said the mother
I ROAR, said the ONE
So they roared and they roared in the sand
in the sun

Over in the meadow in a shed near some sticks
Lived an old mother cow
And her little calves SIX
MOO, said the mother
WE MOO, said the SIX
So they moo'd and they moo'd in the shed
near the sticks

Over in the meadow where the stream
runs so blue
Lived an old mother elephant
And her little calves TWO
STOMP, said the mother
WE STOMP, said the TWO
So they stomped and they stomped where the
stream runs so blue

Over in the meadow where the grass is so even
Lived an old mother mouse
And her little mice SEVEN
SQUEAK, said the mother
WE SQUEAK, said the SEVEN
So they squeaked and they squeaked where the
grass was so even

Over in the meadow in the sky near a tree
Lived an old mother bluebird
And her little bluebirds THREE
FLY, said the mother
WE FLY, said the THREE
So they flew and they flew in the sky near a tree

Over in the meadow by the old mossy gate
Lived a brown mother fox
And her little cubs EIGHT
HUNT, said the mother
WE HUNT, said the EIGHT
So they crept and they crept by the old mossy gate

Over in the meadow in a hive near a door
Lived an old honeybee
And her little bees FOUR
BUZZ, said the mother
WE BUZZ, said the FOUR
So they buzzed and they buzzed in a hive
near the door

Over in the meadow
Where the quiet pools shine
Lived an old mother froggy
And her little froggies NINE
HOP, said the mother
WE HOP, said the NINE
So they hopped and they hopped
Where the quiet pools shine

Over in the meadow in a warren so nice
Lived an old mother rabbit
And her little bunnies FIVE
HOP, said the mother
WE HOP, said the FIVE
So they hopped and they hopped in the
warren so nice

Over in the meadow in the stream round the bend
Lived an old mother fishy
And her little fish TEN
SWIM, said the mother
WE SWIM, said the TEN
So they swam and they swam
In the stream round the bend

Musicaliti Musicaliti

Alice the Camel

Alice the camel had 10 humps
Alice the camel had 10 humps
Alice the camel had 10 humps
So go, Alice, go, boom-boom-boom

Alice the camel had 9 humps
Alice the camel had 9 humps
Alice the camel had 9 humps
So go, Alice, go, boom-boom-boom

Alice the camel had 8 humps
Alice the camel had 8 humps
Alice the camel had 8 humps
So go, Alice, go, boom-boom-boom

Alice the camel had 7 humps
Alice the camel had 7 humps
Alice the camel had 7 humps
So go, Alice, go, boom-boom-boom

Alice the camel had 6 humps
Alice the camel had 6 humps
Alice the camel had 6 humps
So go, Alice, go, boom-boom-boom

Alice the camel had 5 humps
Alice the camel had 5 humps
Alice the camel had 5 humps
So go, Alice, go, boom-boom-boom

Alice the camel had 4 humps
Alice the camel had 4 humps
Alice the camel had 4 humps
So go, Alice, go, boom-boom-boom

Alice the camel had 3 humps
Alice the camel had 3 humps
Alice the camel had 3 humps
So go, Alice, go, boom-boom-boom

Alice the camel had 2 humps
Alice the camel had 2 humps
Alice the camel had 2 humps
So go, Alice, go, boom-boom-boom

Alice the camel had 1 hump
Alice the camel had 1 hump
Alice the camel had 1 hump
So go, Alice, go, boom-boom-boom

Alice the camel had no humps
Alice the camel had no humps
Alice the camel had no humps
Coz Alice is a horse - NEIGH!

Frances Turnbull

Going to the Zoo

Traditional

C
Daddy's taking us to the zoo tomorrow
Zoo tomorrow, zoo tomorrow
C
Daddy's taking us to the zoo tomorrow
We can stay all day

F
We're going to the zoo, zoo, zoo
C
How about you, you, you
G
You can come too, too, too
G   C
We're going to the zoo, zoo, zoo

C
See the elephant with the long trunk swinging
G
Great big ears and long trunk swinging
C
Sniffing up peanuts with the long trunk swinging
G   C
We can stay all day

F
We're going to the zoo, zoo, zoo
C
How about you, you, you
G
You can come too, too, too
C
We're going to the zoo, zoo, zoo

C
See the little monkeys all scritch, scritch, scratching
G
Jumping all around and scritch, scritch, scratching
C
Hanging by their long tails, scritch, scritch, scratching
G   C
We can stay all day

F
We're going to the zoo, zoo, zoo
How about you, you, you
G
You can come too, too, too
C
We're going to the zoo, zoo, zoo

C
We stayed all day and I'm getting sleepy
Sitting in the car getting sleep, sleep, sleepy
C
Home already and I'm sleep, sleep, sleepy
G
Coz we stayed all day

F
We've been to the zoo, zoo, zoo
C
So have you, you, you
You came too, too, too
We've been to the zoo, zoo, zoo

In the Jungle

Traditional

In the jungle
The mighty jungle
The lion sleeps tonight
In the jungle
The mighty jungle
The lion sleeps tonight

A-hee-hee-hee-hee-hee-a-wimba-we
A-hee-hee-hee-hee-hee-a-wimba-we

Near the village
The peaceful village
The lion sleeps tonight
Near the village
The peaceful village
The lion sleeps tonight

A-hee-hee-hee-hee-hee-a-wimba-we
A-hee-hee-hee-hee-hee-a-wimba-we

Hush my darling
Don't fear my darling
The lion sleeps tonight
Hush my darling
Don't fear my darling
The lion sleeps tonight

A-hee-hee-hee-hee-hee-a-wimba-we
A-hee-hee-hee-hee-hee-a-wimba-we

usicaliti

usicaliti

Frances Turnbull

Zulu War Chant

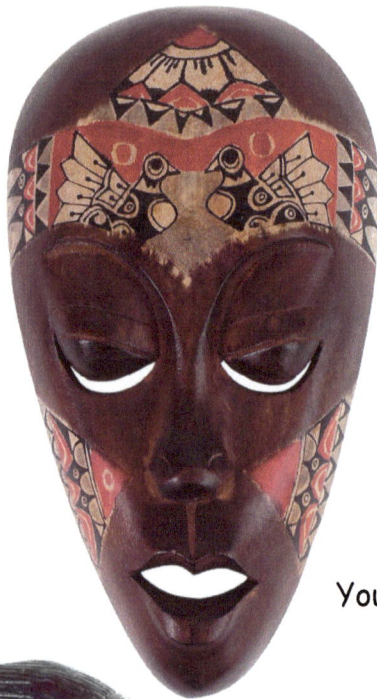

Izika zumba
Zumba, zumba
Izika zumba
Zumba, zay
Izika zumba
Zumba, zumba
Izika zumba
Zumba, zay

Hold him down
You Zulu warrior
Hold him down
You Zulu chief, chief, chief
Hold him down
You Zulu warrior
Hold him down
You Zulu chief, chief, chief

Musicaliti

5 Little Monkeys

Traditional

Five little monkeys jumping on the bed
One fell off and bumped his head
Mummy called the doctor and the doctor said
"No more monkeys jumping on the bed"

Four little monkeys jumping on the bed
One fell off and bumped his head
Mummy called the doctor and the doctor said
"No more monkeys jumping on the bed"

Three little monkeys jumping on the bed
One fell off and bumped his head
Mummy called the doctor and the doctor said
"No more monkeys jumping on the bed"

Two little monkeys jumping on the bed
One fell off and bumped his head
Mummy called the doctor and the doctor said
"No more monkeys jumping on the bed"

One little monkeys jumping on the bed
One fell off and bumped his head
Mummy called the doctor and the doctor said
"No more monkeys jumping on the bed"

I saw your mummy jumping on the bed
She fell off and bumped her head
You called the doctor and the doctor said
"No more MUMMIES jumping on the bed"

musicaliti

Frances Turnbull

How Now Brown Cow

Traditional

How now brown cow
Laaaaaazzzzzyyyy cow!
I'd like to ride a bicycle
But I don't know how
So I chomp the grass
And I swat the flies
And I watch the bicycles
Ride on by

How now brown cow
Laaaaaazzzzzyyyy cow!
I'd like to fly an aeroplane
But I don't know how
So I chomp the grass
And I swat the flies
And I watch the aeroplanes
Fly on by

How now brown cow
Laaaaaazzzzzyyyy cow!
I'd like to drive a steam train
But I don't know how
So I chomp the grass
And I swat the flies
And I watch the steam trains
Chug on by

Musicaliti

Musicaliti

Chipmunk

Anile, anile
Vaa vaa
Azhagiya, anile
Vaa vaa
Goiyya maram, anile
Vaa vaa
Gundu pazham, anile
Vaa vaa
Anile, anile
Vaa vaa

Chipmunk, chipmunk
Come come
Beautiful chipmunk
Come come
Climb high up a
Chipmunk tree
Bring a chipmunk
Back to me
Chipmunk, chipmunk
Come come

Musicaliti

Musicaliti

Frances Turnbull

Sleeping Pets

Traditional

See the little bunnies sleeping
Til it's nearly noon
Come and wake them
With a merry tune
They're so still
Are they ill?
Wake up soon ...

Hop little bunnies
Hop, hop, hop
Hop little bunnies
Hop, hop, hop
Hop little bunnies
Hop, hop, hop
Hop little bunnies
Hop, hop, hop

See the little chipmunks sleeping
Til it's nearly three
Came and wake them
So they can run free
Tap the door
Tap the floor
Wake up soon ...

Run little chipmunks
Run, run, run
Run little chipmunks
Run, run, run
Run little chipmunks
Run, run, run
Run little chipmunks
Run, run, run

Musicaliti

Musicaliti

Brown Horse in the Ring

Traditional

C
There's a brown horse in the ring
C
Tra la la la la
G
There's a brown horse in the ring
C
Tra la la la la la
C
There's a brown horse in the ring
C
Tra la la la la
C   C   G   C
And he looks like a sugar on a plum
PLUM PLUM

C
There's a brown pig in the ring
C
Tra la la la la
G
There's a brown pig in the ring
C
Tra la la la la la
C
There's a brown horse in the ring
C
Tra la la la la
C   C   G   C
And he looks like a sugar on a plum
PLUM PLUM

C
There's a brown sheep in the ring
C
Tra la la la la
C
There's a brown sheep in the ring
C
Tra la la la la la
C
There's a brown horse in the ring
C
Tra la la la la
C   C   G   C
And he looks like a sugar on a plum
PLUM PLUM

Musicaliti

Frances Turnbull

4 White Horses

Traditional

Four white horses
Cross the river
Hey, hey, hey,
Come tomorrow
Come tomorrow
Is a rainy day
Come on and join our
Shadow play
Shadow play is a
Ripe banana
Come on and join our
Shadow play

Four white ponies
Cross the river
Hey, hey, hey,
Come tomorrow
Come tomorrow
Is a rainy day
Come on and join our
Shadow play
Shadow play is a
Ripe banana
Come on and join our
Shadow play

6 Little Ducks

Traditional

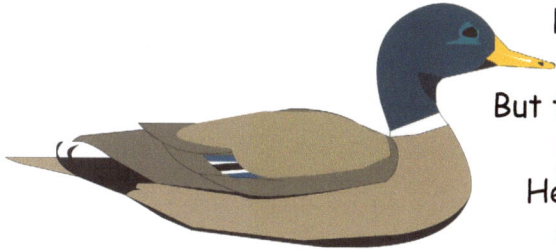

C   G
6 little ducks that I once knew
Fat ones, skinny ones
Fair ones, too
But the one little duck with a
G
Feather on his back
C
He led the others with a
G
Quack, quack, quack
C
Quack, quack, quack
G
Am
Quack, quack, quack
G
He led the others with a
C
Quack, quack, quack

C   G
6 little ducks went out to play
G   C
Over the hills and far away
But the one little duck with a
G
Feather on his back
C
He led the others with a
G
Quack, quack, quack
C
Quack, quack, quack
G
Am
Quack, quack, quack
G
He led the others with a
C
Quack, quack, quack

C   G
6 little ducks that went to sea
G   C
Said that they wanted to play with me
G
But the one little duck with a
G
Feather on his back
C
He led the others with a
G
Quack, quack, quack
C
Quack, quack, quack
G
Am
Quack, quack, quack
G
He led the others with a
C
Quack, quack, quack

Frances Turnbull

Here Comes a Bluebird Traditional

Here comes a bluebird
In through my window
Hey, diddle dum a
Day, day, day
Take a little partner
Jump in the garden
Hey, diddle dum a
Day, day, day

Here comes a sparrow
In through my window
Hey, diddle dum a
Day, day, day
Take a little partner
Skip in the garden
Hey, diddle dum a
Day, day, day

Here comes a pigeon
In through my window
Hey, diddle dum a
Day, day, day
Take a little partner
Prance in the garden
Hey, diddle dum a
Day, day, day

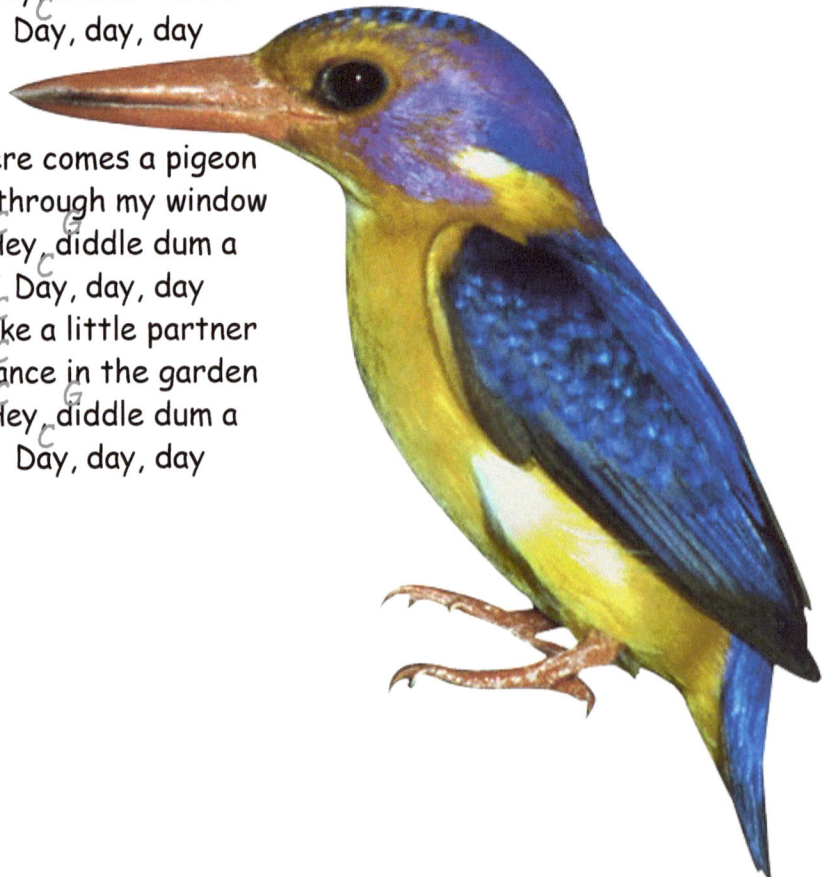

Ladybird

Traditional

Ladybird, ladybird
Fly away home
Your house is on fire
Your children are gone
All except one
And her name is Anne
She crept under
The frying pan

Ladybird, ladybird
Now you are home
Your house has been rescued
Your children are back
Even the one
Whose name is Anne
She crept under
The frying pan

Musicaliti

Musicaliti

Frances Turnbull

3 Little Fishes

Traditional

    C   F   G
Down in the meadow in an itty bitty pool swam
   C   F   G
Three little fishies and a mamma fishy too
      C   F
"Swim" said the mamma fishy
               D
"Swim if you can!" and they
                G
Swam and they swam all over the dam

     C   F   G
Boo, bop, dittem-dattem, whodum, CHOO!
     C   F   G
Boo, bop, dittem-dattem, whodum, CHOO!
     C   F   D
Boo, bop, dittem-dattem, whodum, CHOO!
            G   C
And they swam and they swam all over the dam!

     C   F   G
"Stop!" said the mamma fishy, "or you'll get lost"
      C   F   G
But the 3 little fishies didn't want to be bossed
       C   F
The 3 little fishies went off on a spree
            G   C
And they swam and they swam right out to sea

     C   F   G
Boo, bop, dittem-dattem, whodum, CHOO!
     C   F   G
Boo, bop, dittem-dattem, whodum, CHOO!
     C   F   D
Boo, bop, dittem-dattem, whodum, CHOO!
            G   C
And they swam and they swam right out to sea

     C   F   G
"Whee!" said the little fishies, "here's a lot of fun!"
        C   F   G
"We'll swim in the sea 'til the day is done!"
                      F
They swam and they swam and it was a lark
   C   G
'Til all of a sudden, they saw a shark

     C   F   G
Boo, bop, dittem-dattem, whodum, CHOO!
     C   F   G
Boo, bop, dittem-dattem, whodum, CHOO!
     C   F   D
Boo, bop, dittem-dattem, whodum, CHOO!
            G
'Til all of a sudden, they saw a shark

     C   F   G
"Help!" cried the little fishies, "look at the whale!"
                      F
And quick as they could, they turned on their tails
        C   F
And back to the pool in the meadow they swam
            D   G
And they swam and they swam back over the dam

     C   F   G
Boo, bop, dittem-dattem, whodum, CHOO!
     C   F   G
Boo, bop, dittem-dattem, whodum, CHOO!
     C   F   D
Boo, bop, dittem-dattem, whodum, CHOO!
            G   C
And they swam and they swam back over the dam

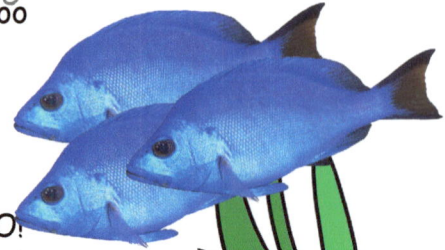

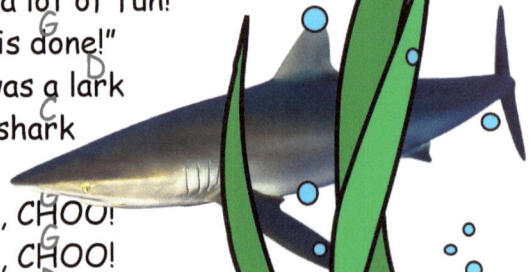

5 Green and Speckled Frogs

Traditional

G
5 green and speckled frogs
Sat on a speckled log
G
Eating the most delicious grubs, yum, yum!
D
One jumped into the pool
C
Where it was nice and cool
G   G
Then there were 4 green speckled frogs

G
4 green and speckled frogs
Sat on a speckled log
G
Eating the most delicious grubs, yum, yum!
D
One jumped into the pool
C
Where it was nice and cool
G   G
Then there were 3 green speckled frogs

G
3 green and speckled frogs
C
Sat on a speckled log
G
Eating the most delicious grubs, yum, yum!
G
One jumped into the pool
C
Where it was nice and cool
G   D   G
Then there were 2 green speckled frogs

G
2 green and speckled frogs
C
Sat on a speckled log
G
Eating the most delicious grubs, yum, yum!
G
One jumped into the pool
C
Where it was nice and cool
G   D   G
Then there was 1 green speckled frog

G
1 green and speckled frog
C
Sat on a speckled log
G
Eating the most delicious grubs, yum, yum!
G
One jumped into the pool
C
Where it was nice and cool
G   G
Then there were no green speckled frogs

Copy or cut out these pictures to use with the tree on page 26 for "Green Grass" (page 8-9).

My Song: _____